Helpers From The Other Realm

Copyright © Angie Clark 2020

ISBN: 978-1-7345576-2-6

Angie Clark Publishing Rockford, Illinois

HELPERS FROM THE OTHER REALM

Angie Clark
Illustrations By: Deon Clark

DEDICATIONS

To My Loving Arch Angels who assist, teaches, guides and protects all who call upon them. To the angelic forces who assist and take action on behalf of righteousness. Respect to our helpers.

CONTENT

ARCH ANGEL ARIEL
Lioness of The Most High
Angel of Nature

ARCH ANGEL CHAMUEL
One Who Sees/Seeks The Most High
Angel of Love

ARCH ANGEL ZADKIEL
Righteousness of The Most High

ARCH ANGEL GABRIEL
Angel of Communication & Revelations
The Gift of Gab

EARTH ANGEL DAMINI
Angel of Harmonious Melodies In Music

ARCH ANGEL RAZIEL
The One Who Knows the Secrets of The Most High

ARCH ANGEL MICHAEL
Chief Commander & Warrior/ Fierce Protector

EARTH ANGEL ANGIEL
Uplifts the Vibrations & Brings out the Best In Others

ARCH ANGEL METATRON
Guardian of The Tree of Life
Scribe of The Most High
The One Who Is Seated Next to The Divine

ARCH ANGEL RAPHAEL
Angel of Healing
Protects Us in Traveling

ARCH ANGEL JOPHIEL
The Beauty & Wisdom of The Most High

ARCH ANGEL JEREMIEL
Mercy of The Most High

ARCH ANGEL RAGUEL
Friend of The Most High

ARCH ANGEL AZRAEL
Angel of Transformation & Death

ARCH ANGEL HANIEL
Angel of Sacred Feminine Energy

ARCH ANGEL URIEL
Fire of The Most High

ARCH ANGEL SANDALPHON
Guardian of The Tree of Life
Carries Our Prayers to The Divine
Angel of Music

ARCH ANGEL MELCHIZEDEK
Angel of Christ Consciousness & Spiritual Evolution
Righteous King of Peace

INTRO

When we call upon the angels and invite them into our presence they become attentive towards us. They initially watch over us, but when we began to interact with them and ask for their assistance, they take action and respond to us in various ways. At times the angels try to get our attention by sending us messages in our dreams, visions, inspired thoughts, intuition, surprise plot twists, healing breakthroughs, answered prayers, revelations, and miracles.

Some characteristics of the angels are similar yet each has their own distinct area they govern over and are responsible for. Some teach, some protect, some supervise, some heal, some helps us to help ourselves, some gives messages to us through dreams, visions, music and inspired thought. Their main goal is to assist us and direct us into a deeper connection with The Divine. The fact that we have free will, the angels intervene only when we are in danger unless we call upon them. We activate them when we call upon them for assistance. The Angels are Supernatural therefore, they will respond to our requests in various ways. At times Angels will appear to us in different forms such as a masculine or feminine energy. Sometimes they answer us and speak to us in ways we may not expect, so it is in our best interest to be aware and to listen to our intuition for guidance.

We may or may not be able to see and hear them. That depends upon the depth of your own supernatural spiritual connection. So, if you feel afraid, stressed, insecure, burdened, and even appreciative let them know. This will increase your relations with them and can grow into a spiritual relationship that brings strength, courage and empowerment beyond your expectations. In this book are only a few of the Arch Angels and Earth Angels, for there are numerous angels. Consider this a introduction into the window of the helpers from the other realm.

ARCH ANGEL ARIEL
Lioness of The Most High
Angel of Nature

Mantra: Magical I Am
Color: Pink Aura
Governs: The care, protection and healing of the animals, earth, water, wind and fire. Aries zodiac sign/ Heart Chakra

- *Helps us to realign with our origin and reminds us of our life purpose*

- *Heightens our psychic powers and awareness of hidden treasures*

- *Embodies a happy abundant spirit overcoming fear and worry*

- *Helps us to set goals and remove obstacles to achieve our desired outcome*

Affirmations: *I appreciate nature and all beings*
- *Abundance flows freely within me*
- *I am happy, aware and encouraged over fear and worry*
- *I accomplish and complete all projects and goals*
- *I am in alignment with divine gifts of prosperity and abundance*

ARCH ANGEL CHAMUEL
The One who Sees/Seeks The Most High
Angel of Love

Mantra: I am loved loving and lovable
Color: Pink Aura
Governs: Hear chakra/ Taurus zodiac sign

- *Activates the heart chakra*
- *Stimulates you to take action*
- *Expands your perception*
- *Inspires self confidence, courage and self esteem*
- *Helps you to make clear sound decisions with a clear sound mind*
- *Helps you to connect with The Divine*
- *Helps you to let go of low vibration habits*
- *Helps you to learn the lessons behind choices, decisions and free will*
- *Helps us to find what was lost*
- *Promotes peaceful harmony within relationships*
- *Bestows sensual abundant pleasures*

Affirmations: *I shift my mind to manifest what I want*
- *I take action with the wisdom of divine guidance*
- *My relationships are peaceful and harmonious*
- *I enjoy the pleasures of life*
- *What was lost is replaced with better*
- *I learn from my past mistakes*
- *My perception is expansive*
- *I love and am loved*

ARCH ANGEL ZADKIEL
Righteousness of The Most High

Mantra: Do the right thing
Color: Dark Royal Blue Aura
Governs: Crown & 3rd eye chakra region/ Gemini zodiac sign

- *Helps us to forgive and let go of painful memories for healing*
- *Improves our memory in reminding us of who we are*
- *Helps us to stay focused on our goals and tasks*
- *Opens us up to our spiritual gifts*
- *Deepens our connection to the Divine*
- *Encourages peace, calmness and love*
- *Enhances our spiritual awakening, awareness and development*

<u>Affirmations:</u> *I let go of pains of the past and forgive as I move towards healing*

- *My memory is clear*
- *I stay focused on my goals and tasks*
- *I use my spiritual gifts productively*
- *I am well connected to the Divine*
- *I am spirituality progressing*

ARCH ANGEL GABRIEL
Angel of Communication & Revelations
Gift of Gab

Mantra: Speech flows through me like rivers of living water
Color: Bronze/Copper & Pearly white aura
Governs: Throat Chakra region/ Cancer zodiac sign

- *Delivers insight and guidance through dreams, visions, inspired thought and intuition*
- *Heals trauma and emotional blockages*
- *Helps you to speak your truth with clarity*
- *Helps you to let go of fears and beliefs of what is blocking you to speak freely and truthful*
- *Helps you to spirituality mature*
- *Encourages communication between ourselves and others to flow smoothly where love and light is felt*

<u>Affirmations:</u> I attract new harmonious healthy friendships with my soul tribe

- *I receive true answers to the questions I ask*
- *I speak my truth wisely*
- *I am growing spirituality*
- *I have authentic communication with others*
- *I listen to my intuition*
- *I am divinely guided*

EARTH ANGEL DAMINI
Angel of Harmonious Melodies in Music
Uplifts Vibrations through Music

Mantra: I sing and dance freely
Color: Yellow/Orange aura
Governs: Heart chakra region/Cancer zodiac sign

- *Uplifts and shifts the energies through harmonious vibes in music and singing*
- *Invokes authenticity within self*
- *Invokes calmness and harmony*

Affirmations: *I vibe and flow in harmony*
- *My life is melodious*
- *I listen to uplifting music*
- *I am authentic*

ARCH ANGEL RAZIEL
The One Who Knows the Secrets of The Most High

Mantra: I am a genius
Color: Rainbow/Clear quartz aura
Governs: Mystical science/Esoteric sage/Crown chakra region/ Leo zodiac sign

- Inspires and enhances creativity
- Gives healing to the psychic, mental and spiritual realm
- Helps us to know the depth of the lessons we face
- Gives knowledge of secret esoteric knowledge
- Enhances spiritual psychic gift awareness such as: telepathy, esp, remote viewing, clairaudience (clear hearing), clairsentience (clear feeling), clairvoyance (clear vision), clairscent (clear smell), clairtangency (clear touch), clairgustance (clear tasting), clairempathy (clear emotion).
- Reveals to us knowledge of the Akasha records/Book of life

<u>Affirmations:</u> I am a mystical genius
- I receive downloads of my Akasha records
- My creativity is expansive and magnified
- My spiritual gifts are enhanced
- I call upon Arch Angel Raziel to bestow me with the gifts of the Holy Spirit
- I use my gifts productively

ARCH ANGEL MICHEAL
Chief Commander Warrior & Fierce Protector
Who is like The Almighty El Shaddai?

Mantra: I am divinely guided and divinely protected

Color: Purple aura

Governs: Throat chakra/ Solar Plexus region/ Leo zodiac sign

- He helps me to free myself from toxic people, places and things
- He encourages me to take action with courage and strength
- He defeats all manner of evil and protects and liberates those who call upon him
- He cuts the cords of unhealthy soul ties and attachments that we are bonded to
- He protects us in our dreams and helps us to remember our dreams
- He calms and gives peace of mind when conflicted

Affirmations: I am calm and protected by Arch Angel Michael
- I am encouraged to take action upon my aspirations
- With the help of Arch Angel Michael I liberate myself from unhealthy attachments
- When I rest I am protected by Arch Angel Michael
- When worried or unsure I call upon Arch Angel Michael for guidance and assistance and he will answer me

EARTH ANGEL ANGIEL
Uplifting the energy
Bestows devotion unto the Divine

Mantra: The Universe is flexible in my favor
Color: Green, silver and white/sky blue aura
Governs: Heart chakra / Crown chakra /
Leo zodiac sign

- *Heightens positive awareness*
- *Assists you to shift your mind to manifest what you want*
- *Invokes a sunny disposition and mood*
- *Promotes equality, fairness and justice*
- *Helps you to heal from trauma and stress*
- *Helps you to connect with the Divine through devotion*
- *Helps you to listen to your intuition*
- *Encourages integrity and dignity*

<u>Affirmations:</u> I am flexible and adaptable
- *I shift my mind to manifest what I want*
- *I am joyful and optimistic*
- *I am successful in all I set out to do*
- *I am highly intuitive*
- *I bring out the best in others*

ARCH ANGEL METATRON
The One who sits next to The Most High
Scribe of The Most High
Guardian of The Tree of Life

Mantra: I am supernaturally gifted
Color: Clear Quartz Crystal
Governs: Sacred geometry(the blueprint and make up of all existence)/Guards the entrance of the Tree of Life/Keeper of The Book of Life/Virgo zodiac sign

- *Helps you to release negative belief patterns and perspectives, old limiting beliefs, vibrations and frequencies*
- *Sage of esoteric knowledge and thought*
- *Resided on Earth as Enoch and transcended as Arch Angel Metatron*
- *He holds the holy scrolls and Akasha records*
- *He guards the Tree of Life entrance*

Affirmations: *I free my mind of negative belief patterns and negative attachments*
- *I use my creative inspiration wisely and productively*
- *My thoughts transcend into higher consciousness*

ARCH ANGEL RAPHAEL
Angel of Healing
Protects those in traveling

Mantra: I am healed
Color: Emerald Green Aura
Governs: 3rd eye region/Gemini & Virgo zodiac sign

- *Healing of the mind body and soul*
- *Heals diseases of spiritual, physical and emotional nature*
- *Restores vitality and strength in health*
- *Helps you to heal relationships by forgiveness and letting go of resentment and negativity*
- *Protects those during travel*

<u>Affirmations:</u> I am protected as I travel
- *I receive healing from arch angel Raphael*
- *I am free of negativity as I focus on being aware and grateful*
- *My relationships are healing*
- *I forgive myself and others*

ARCH ANGEL JOPHIEL
The Beauty and Wisdom of The Most High

Mantra: Wise and beautiful I am
Color: Yellow
Governs: Solar plexus region/ crown chakra/ Libra zodiac sign

- *Helps us to remember our divinity and beauty*
- *Encourages self confidence by activation of the solar plexus chakra region*
- *Sends healing energy to the solar plexus chakra*
- *Helps us to self love and protect our heart*
- *Helps us to connect with the healing powers of flowers*

Affirmations: *I am confident and sure of myself*
- *I am reminded of who I am*
- *Flower power heals me*
- *I let go of pride, arrogance and ignorance as Jophiel teaches me the correct use of my power*
- *I am patient and gentle with myself*

ARCH ANGEL JEREMIEL
Mercy of The Most High

Mantra: I find light in all situations
Color: Dark Purple/Beige and sandy brown
Governs: 3rd eye and Base chakra region

- *Helps us to liberate ourselves when we are feeling stuck or restricted and paralyzed*
- *Helps us to take our power back when we have given it away to others (self love)*
- *Encourages us to move in courage, strength and authority*
- *Assists us in breaking free from past issues for healing*
- *Gives insight into our psychic abilities*
- *Imparts truth and prophecy*
- *Gives us joy and excitement of life*
- *Encourages us to lighten up and be more humorous*

Affirmations: *I move in strength, courage, authority over traumatic issues*
- *I enjoy life and am excited to be in the presence of now*
- *I am light at heart and humorous*
- *My spiritual gifts are used for the highest good of all*
- *I love and believe in myself*
- *I receive truth and prophecy from Arch Angel Jeremiel*

ARCH ANGEL RAGUEL
Friend of The Most High
Angel of Fairness and Justice

Mantra: I am fair and just
Color: Soft ice blue/snow aura
Governs: Solar plexus chakra/ throat chakra

- *He has a calm soothing aura*
- *He supervises other spiritual helpers in the spirit realm*
- *He enforces order, justice and harmony*
- *He promotes fairness and peaceful relationships*
- *He restores order*

Affirmations: *Order and justice is being restored*
- *I call upon Arch Angel Raguel to restore order where there is chaos and disorientation*
- *I am calm and clear minded*
- *I deal with others in fairness*
- *I am encouraged and courageous*

ARCH ANGEL AZRAEL
Angel of Transformation and Death

Mantra: I transform gracefully
Color: Yellow/Creamy vanilla
Governs: Soluna chakra region(top of forehead)
Scorpio zodiac sign

- *Helps us to transform over into the next level of dimension with ease and direction*
- *Helps you when you transition during death of this realm into another realm*
- *He helps to send divine light and healing to the friends and family grieving loss of loved one*

<u>*Affirmations:*</u> *I trust that when I need to transform and transition over Arch Angel Azrael will guide and comfort me to where I need to be*
- *I receive divine light and healing during grief and loss from Arch Angel Azrael*

ARCH ANGEL HANIEL
Angel of Sacred healing energy
Angel of Self Expression

Mantra: I am divine feminine
Color: Turquoise, white and magenta
Governs: The planet Venus and Saturn/The Moon and its cycles/ Third eye chakra/Solar plexus chakra/Sacral chakra
Capricorn zodiac sign

- *Encourages self expression through heightened emotions and feelings of intuition*
- *Gives nurturing, comforting energy as you heal from issues*
- *Helps you to see the beauty in all things*
- *Helps you to heal from neglect, rejection, abandonment and issues like child hood issues*
- *Encourages you to empower yourself and stand in your truth by strengthening your solar plexus chakra*
- *She connects us to the ancient wisdom of the ancestors for healing practices and remedies*

<u>**Affirmations:**</u> *I am healed from deep seated issues*
- *I am well comforted by Haniel as I heal*
- *I love myself*
- *I am empowered and strengthened within*
- *I am connected to my ancestors*

ARCH ANGEL URIEL
The Fire of The Most High

Mantra: I am stable and grounded
Color: Red /yellow aura
Governs: Base and Root chakra/ Aquarius zodiac sign

- Helps to turn disappointments into victory
- Energizes stagnant processes and energies within us
- Holds the scroll of our path and reveals them to us
- Gives us creative insights
- Illuminates and gives clarity when we have lost our way due to feelings of abandonment
  rejection, neglect, despair, suicidal
- Helps us to love and respect ourselves
- Encourages us to overcome our insecurities

__Affirmations:__ My mind is stimulated and activated
- I receive downloads and insight from Arch Angel Uriel
- I give all worries and doubts over to my angels
- I am assisted on how to transcend my mind to create my desires
- I am assisted on how to put my creative ideas into action
- I turn disappointments into victories

ARCH ANGEL SANDALPHON
*Guardian of the exit of The Tree of Life & Earth
Carries our prayers to The Divine*

*Mantra: My prayers reach the threshold of The Most High
Color: Turquoise & Gold
Governs: The exit of the tree of life/ Earth/ Pisces zodiac sign*

- *Sandalphon lived on Earth before as the prophet Elijah and transcended as Arch Angel Sandalphon*
- *He guards the exit of the tree of life and the well being of Earth*
- *Enhances and inspires healing through uplifting music*
- *Helps us to awaken from the trance like state were living in*
- *Takes our prayers to the throne of The Most High*
- *Protects unborn babies in the womb*
- *Helps you to connect deeper with The Divine*

*<u>**Affirmations:**</u> I enjoy healing music*
- *I trust that my prayers reaches the throne of The Almighty*
- *I awaken to truth and clarity*

ARCH ANGEL MELCHIZEDEK
Angel of Christ Consciousness & Spiritual Evolution
Righteous King

- *Self Empowerment*
- *Reveals spiritual truths and esoteric truths*
- *Guards against psychic attacks*
- *Helps in manifestations*
- *Uses therapies for healing and cleansing such as: color therapy, chakra clearing, crystal healing, spiritual releasing, clearing away low/dark energies, correcting unpleasant situations, reiki/ feng shui/ massage*

<u>Affirmations:</u> I manifest easily with no fear no doubt
- *I am strengthened and empowered by Christ within me*
- *I am spiritually wise*
- *I am divinely protected*
- *No weapons formed against me prospers*
- *I am growing and maturing*
- *When I was a child I was childish ,now I am evolving into a wise person*

www.ingramcontent.com/pod-product-compliance
Lightning Source LLC
Chambersburg PA
CBHW070050070426
42449CB00012BA/3211